EXPERIMENTS WITH MAGNETS

A TRUE BOOK

by
Salvatore Tocci

Children's Press®
A Division of Scholastic Inc.

New York Toronto London Auckland Sydney
Mexico City New Delhi Hong Kong
Danbury, Connecticut

A huge magnet picks up metal at an automobile recycling plant.

Reading Consultant
Nanci Vargus
Primary Multiage Teacher
Decatur Township Schools
Indianapolis, Indiana

Science Consultants
Robert Gardner
Former Head of Science Dept.
Salisbury Schools
Salisbury, Connecticut

Kevin Beardmore
Former State Science Coordinator
Indiana Dept. of Education

The author and publisher are not responsible for injuries or accidents that occur during or from any experiments. Experiments should be conducted in the presence of, or with the help of, an adult. Any instructions of the experiments that require the use of sharp, hot, or other unsafe items should be conducted by, or with the help of, an adult.

Library of Congress Cataloging-in-Publication Data

Tocci, Salvatore
    Experiments with magnets / by Salvatore Tocci.
        p. cm. — (A true book)
    Includes bibliographical references and index.
    ISBN 0-516-22248-1 (lib. bdg.) 0-516-27350-7 (pbk.)
    1. Magnets—Experiments—Juvenile literature. 2. Magnetism—Experiments—
Juvenile literature. [1. Magnets—Experiments. 2. Magnetism—Experiments. 3.
Experiments.] I. Title. II. Series.
QC757.5 .T63 2001
538'.078—dc21
                                                                      00-065595

Contents

The word *lodestone* means "leading stone" because it always points, or leads, to the north.

Which Way Is North?

Have you ever used a compass to find out which way is north? Long ago people did not have compasses to help them find their way. Sailors often got lost at sea without them. Then, in the 1200s, sailors discovered how to make a simple compass with a rock called "lodestone."

The sailors hung the lodestone on the end of a string. They then waited to see which way the lodestone turned. They knew that one end of the lodestone would always point toward the north. By knowing which way was north, the sailors could tell in which direction they were sailing. However, the sailors did not know why the lodestone always pointed toward the north.

Why does one end of a lodestone always point north? Why

Have you ever used a magnet to stick something on your refrigerator door?

does a compass point north? You can find the answers to these questions by doing experiments with something that you may already have on your refrigerator door—a magnet.

What Is a Magnet?

A magnet got its name from an area of the world that was once called Magnesia. Today, Magnesia is part of Greece. Lodestone was first discovered in Magnesia almost three thousand years ago. Lodestone contains iron, which is a metal. The iron is what makes the

A straight magnet is called a bar magnet.
Can you identify the horseshoe magnets?

lodestone a magnet. Today magnets made of iron come in many different shapes and sizes.

What exactly is a magnet? A magnet is any object that can attract certain metals. Some metals are strongly attracted by a magnet. Others are weakly attracted or not attracted at all by a magnet. Is there a way to find out how metals are attracted by a magnet?

Attracting Metals

You will need:
- metal objects, such as a piece of aluminum foil, paper fastener, penny, stainless steel spoon, thumbtack, finishing nail, brass screw
- shoe box
- magnet with a hole
- string

Place the metal objects in the shoe box. Tie a piece of string through the hole in the magnet. Slowly pass the magnet over the metal objects. Sort the objects into three groups based on how they are attracted to the magnet—strong, weak, or not at all.

Check out non-metal objects. Find household products made of plastic, glass, wood, rubber, or cardboard. Does a magnet attract any of these non-metal objects?

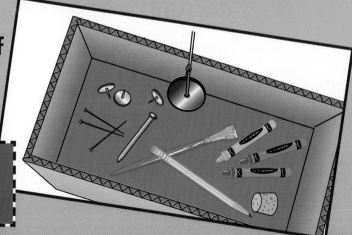

Pass the magnet slowly over the objects in the shoe box.

Thumbtacks and finishing nails are strongly attracted by a magnet.

The thumbtack and finishing nail were strongly attracted to the magnet because they both contain iron. Iron is strongly attracted to a magnet. Iron also makes the best magnet. How can you turn iron into a magnet?

Making a Magnet

You will need:
- bar magnet
- thin iron nail
- finishing nail

Gently stroke one end of a bar magnet against a thin iron nail in the same direction at least twenty-five times. Keep stroking the nail until it is magnetic. Does the iron nail pick up the finishing nail? What other small metal objects will your iron nail attract? Will your iron nail still pick up metal objects tomorrow? Will the nail still pick them up the following day?

You can turn an iron nail into a magnet by rubbing it with another magnet.

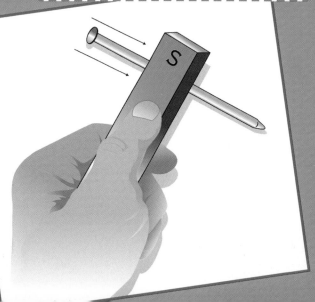

Everything in this picture, including the student, is made of atoms. What other objects shown here are made of atoms?

The iron in lodestone makes the rock a magnet. Why doesn't the iron in a nail make it a magnet? To find the answer, you need to explore something that is too small to see. That is an atom. Everything, including you, is made of atoms.

Imagine if you could see the iron atoms in a magnet. You would see something unusual. All the iron atoms in a magnet would be lined up in the same direction.

Now imagine if you could see the iron atoms in a nail.

The students are lined up in the same direction, just like the atoms in a magnet.

The students are lined up in different directions, just like the atoms in an iron nail.

You would see that the iron atoms in a nail are lined up in different directions. This is why a nail is not a magnet. Rubbing a nail with a magnet forces all the iron atoms to line up in the same direction. The nail then becomes a magnet that can attract other metals. Is there a part of a magnet that attracts best?

Experiment 3

Testing a Magnet

You will need:
• paper clips
• bar magnet

Open a paper clip to form a hook. Stick the hook to one end of a bar magnet. Gently place a paper clip on the hook. How many paper clips will the hook hold before it falls off the magnet?

See how many paper clips you can put on the hook before it falls off the magnet.

Repeat the experiment, but now attach the hook one-half inch from the end of the magnet. How many paper clips does the hook hold? Continue to test the hook by moving it along the magnet, one-half inch at a time. Do this until you reach the other end of the magnet.

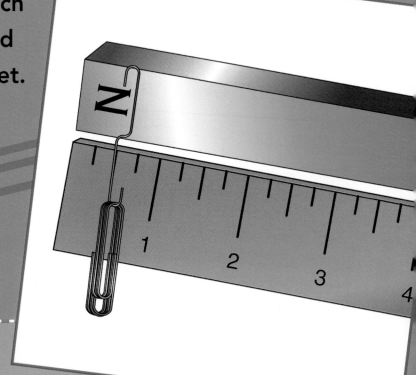

See how many paper clips the hook can hold as you move it along the magnet.

Did you notice that both ends of the bar magnet could hold the most paper clips? The ends of the magnet have the strongest attraction for metal objects. The ends of the magnet are called poles. All magnets have two poles—a north pole and a south pole.

Why Does Lodestone Point North?

The center of the Earth is called the core. The core is made mostly of iron. The temperature in the core is so hot that the iron melts. This melted iron makes the Earth act like a giant magnet with two poles. The Earth's North Pole is in the

The Earth acts like a giant magnet with a north pole and a south pole.

Arctic Circle. The Earth's South Pole is in the Antarctic Circle. How can you figure out that the Earth acts like a giant magnet with two poles?

Experiment 4

Finding the Earth's Poles

You will need:
- small paper clip
- bar magnet
- small cork
- bowl of water

Straighten the paper clip. Rub the paper clip against the bar magnet in the same direction at least twenty-five times. This will make the paper clip magnetic. Keep stroking the paper clip until it is magnetic. Stick a small piece of cork on each end of the paper clip. Float the paper clip in the center of a bowl of water. Notice that the paper clip swings around on the water. One end will point north, and the other end will point south. Turn the paper clip around. Watch what happens.

N

S

The same end of the paper clip will again point north. This end is the north-seeking pole, or simply called the north pole. The other end of the paper clip is the south-seeking pole, or south pole. Your paper clip is not only a magnet but also a compass. Like a lodestone hanging from a string, the paper clip will always point in a north-south direction. The lodestone and the paper clip are magnets that line up with the Earth's two poles.

You now know that one end of a bar magnet is its north pole. The other end is its south pole. You also know that the poles have the strongest attraction for some metal objects. However, where are the poles on magnets that are shaped differently, like a horseshoe magnet?

Finding a Magnet's Poles

You will need:
- steel wool pad
- sheet of paper
- horseshoe magnet

Pull apart a steel wool pad into very small pieces. Put the pieces on a sheet of paper. Hold the paper with one hand. With your other hand, pass the magnet back and forth under the paper. Watch what happens to the pieces of steel wool.

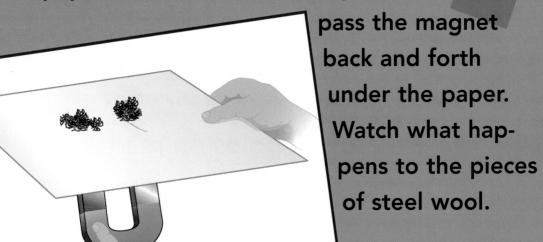

The steel wool pieces are attracted mostly by the two ends of the magnet.

One of the metals in steel is iron. The two ends of a horseshoe magnet attract the iron in the steel wool. The ends of the magnet must be the two poles. The north pole of a magnet, however, is very different from its south pole. How is the south pole different from the north pole?

Experiment 6

Comparing the Poles

You will need:
- steel wool pad
- sheet of paper
- two bar magnets

Break apart a steel wool pad into tiny pieces. Place the pieces in a pile on a sheet of paper. Dip the north pole of a bar magnet into the pieces. Dip the south pole of another bar magnet into the pieces. Over the paper, hold the first magnet's north pole against the second magnet's south pole.

The north pole and south pole attract each other.

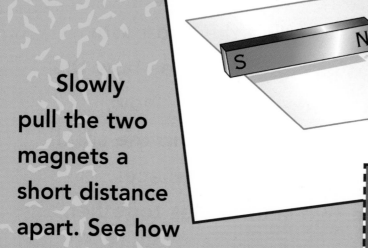

Slowly pull the two magnets a short distance apart. See how the metal pieces hang in the air between the two magnets.

The attraction between the two poles keeps the steel wool pieces hanging in the air.

There is a strong attraction between the north pole of one magnet and the south pole of another magnet. Opposite poles attract each other. This attraction is so strong that it keeps the metal pieces hanging in the air.

Remove the steel wool pieces from the magnets and place them in a pile. This time, dip the north poles of both magnets into the pile. Then try to bring the two north poles together over the paper. See how the two poles push each other apart. Now, remove the steel wool pieces. Dip the south poles of both magnets into the pieces. Slowly bring the two south poles together.

If the two poles are the same, they will push each other apart. This causes the steel wool pieces on one magnet to move away from the pieces on

Two identical poles push each other away. Notice how the steel wool pieces are clustered around each of the poles.

the other magnet. Is there anything else magnets can do besides attract and push apart metal objects, like the pieces of steel wool?

What Else Can Magnets Do?

Magnets have been found to have other uses. For example, most of the electricity we use to power televisions, computers, and other devices depends on magnets. Also, most power plants use huge magnets to make electricity. How can a magnet make electricity?

These power generators inside the
Hoover Dam in Las Vegas, Nevada, use
huge magnets to make electricity.

Experiment 7

Making Electricity

You will need:
- flashlight
- compass
- 6 feet of insulated copper wire
- narrow drinking glass or jar
- plastic twist ties
- bar magnet

Turn on the flashlight. Electricity from the batteries causes the bulb to light. Slowly pass the flashlight near the compass. Notice how the needle turns. Electricity also causes the compass needle to turn.

Now, wrap about 6 feet of the copper wire around a narrow glass or jar. Leave about 10 inches of wire free at both ends. Slide the wire from the glass. Wrap plastic twist ties around the wire so that it makes a thick, tight coil. Wrap one end of the wire around the compass in the same

direction that the
needle is point-
ing. Now wrap
the other end of
the wire around
the compass in the
same way.

Hold the coil of
wire with one hand.
With your other
hand, slide a bar
magnet inside the
coil's center.

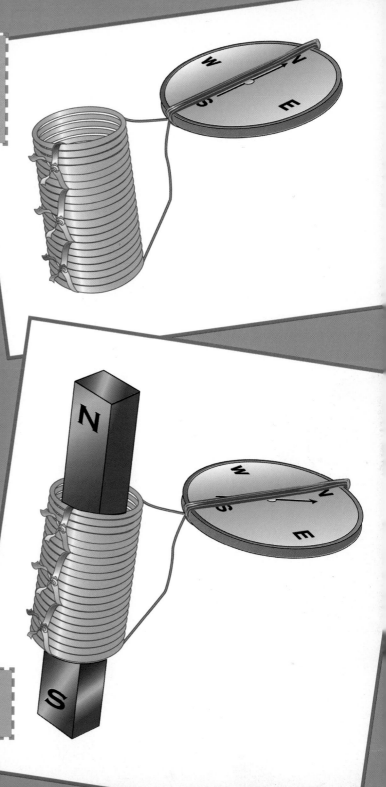

Watch the compass needle. Does the needle respond to the magnet? Now, move the magnet quickly in and out of the coil's center. Notice that the needle turns each time the magnet is moved. The magnet makes electricity flow through the wire. This electricity causes the needle to turn, just like electricity from the flash- light batteries made the needle turn.

Magnets are powerful enough to lift this train and move it above its tracks.

Large magnets are also used to lift objects, even heavy ones. There are several ways that magnets lift heavy objects. One way is to use two magnets. How can you make one magnet lift another magnet?

Lifting a Magnet

You will need:
- two bar magnets of the same size
- piece of foam
- six pencils

Trace the outline of a bar magnet on a piece of foam. Remove the magnet.

Gently push the pencils into the outline on the foam.

Place the six pencils so that the bar magnet will fit between them.

Lower the bar magnet between the pencils so that it rests on the foam. Then gently lower another bar magnet between the pencils.

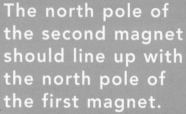
The north pole of the second magnet should line up with the north pole of the first magnet.

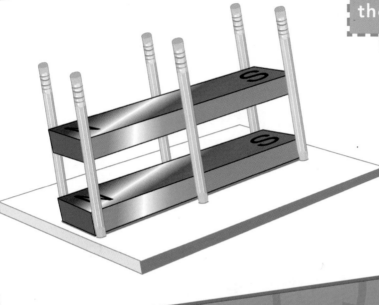

Make sure that the north pole of the second magnet is over the north pole of the first magnet. The poles of the two magnets push away from each other. The second magnet will float over the first one. If you have more magnets, see what happens when you add them. Be sure to line up the north poles.

Magnets are used for a variety of reasons. One is to make compasses. A compass is a magnet with both north and south poles. Today sailors realize that a compass needle does not point directly to the Earth's North Pole. The needle points to a spot near the North Pole. This spot is known as the North Magnetic Pole and is located in northern Canada.

Fun With Magnets

Now that you've learned some things about magnets, here's a fun experiment to do.

You can use what you know about a magnet's poles to do a magic trick.

Experiment 9

Performing Magic

You will need:
- four empty, small cardboard boxes or soap boxes
- two small bar magnets that fit inside the boxes
- masking tape

Tape a small bar magnet to the inside of a cardboard box or soap box. Do this again with a second magnet and box. Stand the boxes on end, about three inches apart. Make sure that the north poles of both magnets are at the top ends. Slowly move one box toward the other. Before they touch, the second box should get knocked over. This happens because the two north poles push each other away.

Stand the two boxes on end. This time, however, have the opposite poles face each other. As you slowly move one box toward the other one, the two of them should come together before they touch. The opposite poles attract each other. Now ask your friends to try it. However, be sure to give them two boxes that do not have magnets inside them.

To Find Out More

If you would like to learn more about magnets, check out these additional resources.

 **Books**

Levine, Shar. **Magnet Book**. Sterling Publishing Co., 1998.

Nankivell-Aston, Sally, and Dorothy Jackson. **Science Experiments with Magnets.** Franklin Watts, 2000.

Vecchione, Glen. **Magnet Science.** Sterling Publishing Co., 1995.

Organizations and Online Sites

The Baken Museum
3537 Zenith Avenue South
Minneapolis, MN
55416-4623
612-927-6508
http://www.bakenmuse-um.org/

This is a center for learning that deals only with electricity and magnetism. You can visit an image gallery and contact them for publications, programs, and kits that deal with magnets.

National Museum of Science and Technology
PO Box 9724, Station T
Ottawa, ON K1G 5A3
Canada
613-991-3044
http://www.science-tech.nmstc.ca/english/contactus/index.cfm

Type in the key word "magnets" in the search box and you will be led to several activities that you can do with magnets.

The Exploratorium
3601 Lyon Street
San Francisco, CA 94123
415-397-5673
http://www.exploratorium.edu/snacks/snackintro.html

Log on to their site to see how you can carry out experiments using magnets. This site has a list of "snacks" that are miniature versions of hands-on exhibits at the museum. One "snack" shows you how to make a magnetic force that is stronger than the Earth's.

45

Important Words

atom the smallest particle that makes up you or anything else

compass a tool with a magnetic needle that points to the north

core the Earth's center that is made of melted iron

lodestone a rock that contains iron and acts like a magnet

magnet an object that attracts certain metals

pole part of a magnet that has the strongest attraction for certain metals

steel a metal made by mixing iron with other metals

Index

Meet the Author

Salvatore Tocci is a science writer who lives in East Hampton, New York, with his wife, Patti. He was a high school biology and chemistry teacher for almost thirty years. As a teacher, he always encouraged his students to do experiments to learn about science. When he is not writing, he and his wife spend much of their time sailing their boat, the *Royal T*, on which they have a compass to direct them safely across the sea.

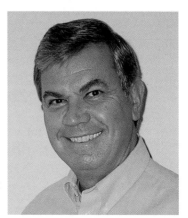

Photographs ©: Corbis-Bettmann/Pablo Corral: 7; FPG International/VCG: 12; Fundamental Photos: 2 (Wayne Decker), cover (Richard Megna), 4 (Paul Silverman); Nance S. Trueworthy: 15, 16; PhotoEdit: 37 (Apollo), 9, 33 (Tony Freeman), 1 (Richard Hutchings); Stone: 21; Visuals Unlimited: 19 (John Sohlden), 14 (Jeff Greenberg).

Illustrations by Michael DiGiorgio